Original title:
Skylines and Sonnets

Copyright © 2024 Creative Arts Management OÜ
All rights reserved.

Author: Clement Portlander
ISBN HARDBACK: 978-9916-88-064-7
ISBN PAPERBACK: 978-9916-88-065-4

Chasing Shadows in the City

In alleyways where secrets lie,
Flickering lights paint the night sky.
Footsteps echo, a haunting sound,
Chasing shadows that dance around.

Underneath the buzzing signs,
Dreams collide as life entwines.
A whisper here, a laugh goes by,
Seeking truth as moments fly.

Harmonies of Iron and Sky

Steel and glass rise towards the blue,
Voices meld in a vibrant hue.
Machines hum a tireless song,
Where every note feels right or wrong.

Winds carry tales from the past,
A city's heart beats bold and fast.
With each echo, life's rhythm sways,
In this symphony of endless days.

Verses at Dusk

As day retreats, the sky ignites,
Colors blend into starry nights.
A soft embrace of twilight's grace,
Time slows down, a gentle pace.

Whispers linger, like soft sighs,
Painting dreams across the skies.
With every heartbeat, stories flow,
In the warmth of the evening glow.

Silver Linings Over Concrete

Amidst the gray, a shimmer waits,
Life's richness found in simple states.
Through cracks in stone, flowers bloom,
Resilience thrives, dispelling gloom.

Each silver lining, a spark of hope,
In the city's arms, we learn to cope.
With every dawn, a chance renews,
Embracing life's myriad hues.

Elysium of Echoed Words

In twilight's glow, whispers dance,
Echoed secrets in a trance.
Each word a star, they take their flight,
Painting dreams in the velvet night.

In the garden where thoughts bloom,
Every moment, dispelling gloom.
A symphony wrapped in tender sighs,
Elysium sings where magic lies.

Luminescent Lines

With every stroke, the canvas glows,
A tapestry where passion flows.
Bright colors weave a tale untold,
Luminescent lines, a sight to behold.

In the silence, visions weave,
Stories blossom, hearts believe.
Each stroke a heartbeat in the dark,
Illuminating dreams that spark.

Soliloquy in the Sky

Beneath the vast expanse so clear,
Whispers of the cosmos near.
A soliloquy that floats on high,
Where thoughts take wing and freely fly.

Stars listen close to heartfelt cries,
As moonlight speaks and never lies.
In the stillness, wisdom flows,
A dialogue where the universe knows.

Architecture of Emotion

In every heart, a structure stands,
Built with hope by gentle hands.
Walls of laughter, windows of tears,
Architecture shaped by all our years.

Foundations laid in love's embrace,
Each corner whispers of our grace.
In shadows cast, the heart reveals,
The beauty found in what it feels.

The Untold Stories Above

Whispers of stars glow bright at night,
They weave tales of dreams and lost flight.
In the silence, secrets softly bloom,
As galaxies spin in their vast room.

Clouds cradle thoughts we dare not share,
Floating away with a gentle prayer.
Above the noise, we yearn to see,
The stories told between you and me.

Comets race, leaving trails of light,
Echoing paths in the darkened night.
Each flicker a memory, flickering fast,
Reminders of moments that fade but last.

So when you gaze at the endless sky,
Remember the tales that softly lie.
Among the stars, our hopes align,
In the universe's embrace, we intertwine.

A Journey Through Urban Echoes

In the city's heart, where sidewalks hum,
Voices collide, each moment's drum.
Neon lights paint stories bright,
As shadows dance in the fall of night.

Skyscrapers whisper of dreams anew,
Concrete giants with a view askew.
Every turn holds a secret gaze,
Lost in the maze of urban ways.

Trains rumble by, a daily refrain,
Carrying lives through joy and pain.
Through the chaos, a rhythm beats,
A symphony of life on bustling streets.

In this tapestry woven tight,
We find our place in the city's light.
Each echo a step in our song,
Together we wander, where we belong.

Poetry Carried by the Wind

Listen closely to the gentle breeze,
It carries whispers among the trees.
Each flurry a line from nature's pen,
Writing tales of now, and when.

Songs of the past dance on the air,
Tales of love, of joy, and despair.
Leaves flutter down, a soft refrain,
In every rustle, a story remains.

Across the fields, where wildflowers sway,
The wind recites what words cannot say.
In its breath, we find our voice,
Together with nature, we rejoice.

So let your heart soar and your spirit bend,
To the poetry carried by the wind.
Embrace the verses the world confides,
In the symphony of life, love abides.

Magic in the Air

Whispers float on gentle breeze,
Stars above begin to tease.
Moonlight dances on the ground,
In this magic, joy is found.

Fireflies paint the evening's glow,
Casting dreams that softly flow.
Hearts entwined in silent sighs,
Wonders gleam in open eyes.

Echoes of a world unknown,
Every moment sparkled, shone.
Through the night, we'll wander far,
Chasing dreams beneath the stars.

Cityscapes of Emotion

Concrete towers scrape the sky,
Steel and glass, oh how they fly.
Every street holds stories told,
Whispers of the brave and bold.

Neon lights in vibrant hues,
Painting paths for wandering shoes.
Cafés filled with laughter's cheer,
Silent sorrows linger near.

In every corner, life unfolds,
Memories in bricks and molds.
City heartbeats pulse and race,
In the chaos, find your place.

Dreams on the Edge

Balancing on a fragile line,
Where the heart and mind align.
Hopes like whispers in the night,
Guiding dreams towards the light.

Every breath a leap of faith,
Chasing visions we create.
Through the shadows, shadows play,
Boldly stepping into day.

Mountains rise and rivers flow,
Emotions high and spirits low.
Yet we dare, we reach, we climb,
In the dusk, we spark the time.

The Pulse of the Night Sky

Stars align in cosmic dance,
Winking fate, a fleeting chance.
Galaxies spin in sweet perfume,
Breathless magic in the gloom.

Night unfolds like velvet drapes,
While the world in stillness shapes.
Every heartbeat echoes wide,
In the dark where dreams reside.

Celestial whispers call us near,
Filling hearts with love and fear.
Underneath this vast expanse,
We find our place in night's romance.

City Dreams

In the glow of neon lights,
Hopes and wishes intertwine,
Sidewalks whisper secrets told,
In each shadow, dreams unfold.

Skyscrapers touch the endless night,
Stars above, a distant sight,
Each heartbeat echoes, wild and free,
In this bustling symphony.

Voices blend in harmony,
Stories of both you and me,
In every corner, life anew,
City dreams are born and grew.

As the dawn begins to break,
Awakening with every wake,
We chase the light, in hope we rise,
In these city dreams, our skies.

Verses Under Twilight

Beneath the sky of fading blue,
Whispers dance in shadows' hue,
Night's embrace, a gentle balm,
In twilight's grip, we find our calm.

Stars emerge, a silver lace,
In the quiet, we find grace,
Silhouettes against the glow,
In this moment, time moves slow.

Voices linger, soft and clear,
Every laugh and every tear,
Captured in the twilight mist,
In this world, none can be missed.

As night unfolds its velvet art,
Each flicker warms a restless heart,
Together woven, we align,
In verses sweet, our dreams entwine.

Urban Echoes

Among the concrete towers high,
Echoes of a city sigh,
Footsteps patter on the stone,
In this place, we are not alone.

Sirens wail, a distant song,
In the rhythm, we belong,
Every corner tells a tale,
In urban night, we set our sail.

Windows glimmer, stories shared,
In the silence, voices dared,
Together in the bustling throng,
In every heartbeat, life is strong.

Through the streets, we wander lost,
In the echo, find the cost,
Yet joy persists, a flame that glows,
In urban echoes, love still grows.

Lines Above the Horizon

In the dawn, the colors blend,
Lines of hope that never end,
Golden rays embrace the day,
In their warmth, our fears allay.

Clouds drift softly, dreams unfurl,
With each sunrise, we may twirl,
Brush the sky with thoughts so bright,
In these lines, we find our light.

Mountains stand, proud and tall,
Guardians of the stories' call,
With each step, we rise above,
In pursuit of peace and love.

When twilight falls, and stars ignite,
Lines above hold dreams in flight,
Chasing shadows, we believe,
In this journey, we achieve.

The Bridge Between Worlds

In twilight hush, the shadows blend,
A path between what bends and mends.
Whispers travel on the breeze,
As time reveals the secrets' ease.

The stars align, a bridge is spun,
Connecting dreams, each heart has won.
With every step, the borders fade,
In symphony, new worlds are made.

A silent promise held in air,
A dance of hope in moonlight's glare.
Each heartbeat, a rhythm of grace,
In this realm, we find our place.

So take my hand, let's drift away,
Into the dawn of a brand new day.
We cross the bridge with gentle sighs,
Embracing love beneath the skies.

Heights of Imagination

Upon the clouds, our thoughts take flight,
Escaping chains of day and night.
With every dream, we soar so high,
Touching the limitless, vast sky.

In realms unseen, where wishes grow,
Ideas bloom in radiant flow.
Canvas spun from vivid hues,
Crafting worlds that we can choose.

Mountains made of hopes and fears,
Each summit climbs through laughter, tears.
The heights we reach define our quest,
In every heart, a story pressed.

So venture forth, let visions soar,
In heights of imagination, explore.
With every step, our spirits thrive,
In this vast world, we are alive.

Urban Reflections at Sunset

Golden rays drape the city's core,
As shadows stretch and spirits soar.
Reflections dance on glassy panes,
In silent whispers, the city reigns.

The streets alive with tales untold,
Each corner hides a heart of gold.
In every glance, a story flows,
Where joy and sorrow interrose.

With sunset's brush, the skyline glows,
Painting dreams where the river flows.
A symphony of light and sound,
In urban heartbeats, life is found.

As day gives way to evening's sigh,
The city breathes a soft goodbye.
In twilight's embrace, we understand,
In urban reflections, we stand hand in hand.

The Dance of Lights

In the night, the stars ignite,
Drawing patterns of pure delight.
A cosmic waltz in velvet skies,
Where whispers echo, softly rise.

Lanterns flicker with gentle grace,
Guiding hearts through time and space.
Each beam a step in rhythmic play,
In the dance of lights, night finds its way.

Colors blend on the silent floor,
Creating dreams we can explore.
With every twinkle, magic blooms,
As shadows weave through darkened rooms.

So let us twirl in this embrace,
In the dance of lights, we find our place.
Together, lost in spark and flame,
A timeless bond, a glowing name.

Stanzas of Steel and Glass

In shadows cast by towers tall,
Reflections dance on bustling streets,
The heartbeat of the city calls,
Where dreams and concrete often meet.

With every stride on pavement laid,
The stories whisper, intertwine,
In each facade, a life portrayed,
A symphony of steel and spine.

Above, a sky of cobalt blue,
Framed by the glass, it seems to gleam,
A vibrant tale of the city's hue,
In every window, hope and dream.

Yet in the night, when silence falls,
The moonlight streams through every crack,
In stanzas formed by steel's embrace,
We find our paths, we find our track.

A Symphony of Skylights

Beneath the arch of urban skies,
The sunlit dance of beams and light,
A symphony of hope that flies,
Where shadows blend with brilliance bright.

Glass and metal, a grand design,
Each structure sings a song profound,
In harmony, the stars align,
As dreams awaken all around.

The rooftops host a quiet grace,
A stage for thoughts that soar and swell,
In every angle, every space,
Lies a story yet to tell.

With each new dawn, the world ignites,
An azure canvas, fresh and free,
A symphony of skylights bright,
Where we can be what we can be.

Beneath the Canopy of Skyscrapers

Beneath the tallest spires we roam,
In shadows deep, we seek our way,
The city fabric feels like home,
With whispered dreams both night and day.

Concrete giants touch the sky,
Their forms an echo of our fate,
As we raise voices up high,
In unity, we celebrate.

The light that filters through the steel,
Creates a canvas, warm and bright,
In every heartbeat, we can feel,
The pulse of life, the joy, the fight.

Beneath the watchful towers' gaze,
We stand together, bold and true,
In this embrace, we find our phase,
Beneath the vast and endless blue.

The Poetics of Urban Heights

In urban heights, a skyline dreams,
Where poets walk the crowded lanes,
Each breath a verse, each glance it seems,
Is woven into city chains.

With buildings reaching for the stars,
And lights that blink like distant eyes,
We write our tales from near and far,
In whispers carried on the sighs.

A tapestry of lives engaged,
In every corner, life unfolds,
With every heartache, every wage,
A narrative that never grows old.

The poetics swell in every street,
A rhythm marked by hope and stress,
Where art and life so deftly meet,
In urban heights, our lives express.

The Poetry of Dawn

Whispers of light break the night,
Colors awaken, a beautiful sight.
Birds sing their songs, a gentle embrace,
Nature unfolds with grace and pace.

The horizon blushes, a canvas anew,
Mysteries unveil in the morning dew.
Dreams linger softly, as shadows retreat,
A new day begins, life feels complete.

Golden rays dance on fields of green,
A world reborn, vibrant and serene.
Hope ignites in the heart's quiet space,
A moment of peace, a sacred place.

Dawn's gentle touch inspires the soul,
Renewal emerges, making us whole.
With each new sunrise, we start again,
Embracing the beauty, letting love reign.

Reflections in the Air

Clouds drift like thoughts on a gentle breeze,
Thoughts of the past, drifting with ease.
Mirrored in skies, memories take flight,
In the dance of the day, both dark and light.

Whispers of wind carry secrets untold,
Stories of ages, both tender and bold.
Cascading echoes of laughter and tears,
Floating like bubbles, unmarked by years.

In the vast expanse, we search for our place,
Finding reflections, a glimpse of our grace.
With each fleeting moment, a chance to renew,
The air holds our dreams, painted in blue.

Voices in harmony weave through the air,
Bonds of connection, a love we all share.
Each breath is a promise, a vow in the sky,
Together we rise, as the moments pass by.

Glass Gardens

In gardens of glass where colors collide,
Fragile reflections in silence reside.
Petals like prisms, both vibrant and clear,
Nature's enchantment whispers near.

Beams of sunlight dance on each shard,
Creating a beauty, both bold and starred.
With every glimpse, a fragile allure,
In this world of glass, our hearts feel secure.

Rain showers softly, a melody sweet,
Kissing the surfaces, where dreams and reality meet.
Each droplet glistens like tears of delight,
In these glass gardens, everything feels right.

As evening descends, the shadows will play,
Transforming the glass into night's soft array.
Within this magical, shimmering space,
We find our reflections, in love's sweet embrace.

The Tune of Towers

In the shadow of towers reaching high,
Whispers of dreams float up to the sky.
Each brick and beam tells a story untold,
Echoes of past, both timid and bold.

The streets below hum with life and cheer,
A symphony echoes, both distant and near.
Voices of strangers, a blend in the crowd,
Together they stand, both humble and proud.

As twilight descends, windows aglow,
The tune of the towers begins to flow.
Harmony dances in rhythm and rhyme,
A clock that ticks forward, defying all time.

In the heart of the city, where dreams intertwine,
The song of the towers, eternally shine.
With each passing moment, let our spirits soar,
To the tune of the towers, forevermore.

Echoes in the Urban Abyss

Cold shadows play in dim-lit streets,
Footsteps echo in hurried retreats.
Concrete towers loom above,
Whispers of dreams, the city of love.

Lost souls wander, searching for light,
In the abyss where day meets night.
Voices rise, drowning in noise,
Hope entwined with the city's poise.

Neon glows, a flicker of dreams,
Laughter and sorrow in moonlit beams.
Memory lingers in every crack,
In the abyss, there's no looking back.

Yet among the chaos, hearts still beat,
Finding solace in the city's heat.
In echoes that linger, the night takes flight,
In the urban abyss, we embrace the night.

Voices of the High-rise

Windows framed by dreams and despair,
High above, souls find their air.
Concrete jungles, peaks of ambition,
Voices rise with clear definition.

The hum of life in crowded halls,
Whispers shared on echoing walls.
A tapestry woven of hopes and fears,
Together we stand, through laughter and tears.

Elevator rides bring stories anew,
Each floor a chapter, every heart true.
In the heights we flourish and strive,
Voices united, this city's alive.

From skyline views, we behold the spree,
In the heart of the high-rise, we long to be free.
A symphony played on concrete strings,
Voices of the high-rise, the joy it brings.

Rooftop Reveries

Above the city, a world to explore,
Rooftop dreams with an open door.
Stars come alive, whispering tales,
In the night sky, our spirit prevails.

Sipping dreams under moonlit skies,
The city glows, a treasure in lies.
Moments linger, the breeze like a song,
On rooftops we find where we belong.

Glimpses of life through distant haze,
A canvas painted in twilight's rays.
Conversations float like smoke in the air,
In rooftop reveries, we shed our care.

As dawn breaks softly, a gentle embrace,
The world awakens, a familiar face.
Yet we'll cherish these heights we adore,
In rooftop reveries, we always want more.

Starlit Spaces

Under the blanket of endless night,
Starlit spaces feel so right.
A cosmic dance above our heads,
While dreams awaken from their beds.

Whispers of wonder in the cosmic sea,
Each star a wish, each wish a plea.
Guided by light, we search the vast,
In starlit spaces, we're free at last.

Time pauses here, beneath the glow,
In silence, the universe begins to flow.
Infinite beauty, a gentle embrace,
In these starlit spaces, we find our place.

Hearts intertwined with the celestial tide,
In the quiet of night, our fears subside.
Forever in awe of the cosmic dance,
In starlit spaces, we take a chance.

Whispers of Steel and Stone

In the city, shadows creep,
Beneath the echoes, secrets keep.
Cold metal sings in the night,
While history glows with fading light.

A watchtower gazes far and wide,
Guarding tales of those who tried.
Brick and mortar, stories told,
In the silence, dreams unfold.

The pulses of life, a rhythmic beat,
Walking paths where souls would meet.
Rust and dust, a silent fight,
In the whispers of steel, there's light.

A gentle touch of rain's descent,
Awakens ghosts of dreams misspent.
In every corner, shadows blend,
Steel and stone, the world transcends.

High Above the Horizon

Where the sky meets the sea,
Clouds dance wild and free.
Colors burst at dusk's embrace,
Nature's canvas, a vast space.

Mountains rise, their peaks aglow,
Kissed by rays, a golden show.
Winds whisper through the trees,
Carrying tales on the breeze.

Stars awaken, dreams ignite,
In the dark, they share their light.
Horizons stretch, a boundless view,
Every shade, a story new.

Above the world, we find our place,
Lost in beauty, a warm grace.
The sun dips low, a final run,
Daylight fades, but hopes are spun.

The Poetry of Twilight

Twilight lingers, soft and deep,
Crickets chirp while others sleep.
Shadows lengthen, colors merge,
In soft whispers, emotions surge.

Glimmers of gold in fading light,
Twilight dances, a sweet sight.
Stars peek out, their secrets shared,
In this moment, none are scared.

The world slows down, time stands still,
Every heart beats, a gentle thrill.
Petals close, embracing the night,
In twilight's arms, all feels right.

A poem written in every hue,
In silence, we find the true.
As shadows wane, a promise gleams,
In twilight's poetry, we dream.

Rooftops and Reflections

Above the city, birds take flight,
Rooftops gleam in the fading light.
Windows shimmer, stories blend,
In every pane, lives extend.

Quiet corners, a hidden grace,
Chasing echoes, a fast-paced race.
Shared smiles and soft goodbyes,
In the sky, our hope still flies.

From high above, the world feels small,
Each rooftop whispers, answers call.
Reflections dance on glassy streams,
In every glimpse, there's space for dreams.

With stars above and streets below,
Rooftops hold what we all know.
In the night, we look and see,
Reflections of who we can be.

Lyrical Horizons

Beyond the hills, the sun does rise,
A canvas spread across the skies.
With whispers soft, the breeze does dance,
Inviting all to dream and glance.

Mountains high, in shadows framed,
Each peak and vale, forever named.
A palette bright, of colors bold,
A timeless tale, in hues retold.

The rivers flow in gentle grace,
Reflecting light, a warm embrace.
Each ripple sings, a song of peace,
In nature's arms, all worries cease.

As twilight falls, the stars ignite,
A tapestry of day turns night.
With every breath, the world aligns,
In lyrical horizons, life entwines.

Urban Odes

In concrete towers, dreams take flight,
Beneath the glow of city light.
Each bustling street, a tale to tell,
In whispered moments, all is well.

The laughter echoes, spirits rise,
A harmony beneath the skies.
With every step, a rhythm found,
In melodies that wrap around.

The vibrant art, on walls displayed,
A pulse of life, none can evade.
In every corner, stories bloom,
Urban odes that chase the gloom.

The night unveils its sparkling charm,
With every heartbeat, a warm balm.
A symphony of hearts aligned,
In city's grasp, our dreams entwined.

Glimmers Above the City

On rooftop heights, where silence breaks,
The stars descend, the city wakes.
With every twinkle, hope ignites,
A tapestry of shared delights.

The skyline gleams, a silver thread,
Weaving dreams, from night to bed.
Each breath of air, a whispered prayer,
Glimmers above, beyond compare.

The moon ascends, a watchful eye,
Reflecting all, as hours fly.
In gentle waves, the night unfolds,
Unraveling stories, yet untold.

As dawn approaches, shadows fade,
In golden light, new paths are laid.
With every sunrise, hopes anew,
Glimmers above, a guiding view.

Urban Reverie

In the heart of streets, dreams collide,
Where stories linger, hopes abide.
Each corner turned, a new refrain,
In urban reverie, joy and pain.

The trains that rush, the people flow,
A vibrant dance, in ebb and glow.
The city's pulse, a steady beat,
With every step, life feels complete.

The cafes hum with laughter's song,
In moments shared, we all belong.
With every smile, a bond is spun,
In urban realms, we're all as one.

As twilight casts its velvet hue,
The city shimmers, fresh and new.
In dreams we weave, a tapestry,
In urban reverie, we feel free.

Horizons of Hope

In dawn's embrace, the light unfurls,
A canvas bright, where dreams can swirl.
Each step we take, a path anew,
Horizons gleam in shades of blue.

With every heartbeat, courage grows,
Through winds of change, the spirit flows.
In every star that twinkles high,
Hope's gentle whisper never dies.

The morning mist, a veil of grace,
Awakens strength we all must face.
While shadows dance, the sun will rise,
In tender light, our future lies.

Luminescent Whispers

Beneath the night, the fireflies glow,
Whispers of magic in twilight's flow.
Their gentle light, a secret shared,
In silent dreams, our souls bared.

The moonlit path, a guide to find,
Illuminates thoughts within the mind.
Each flicker speaks of tales untold,
Of love and loss, both brave and bold.

Through leaves that rustle, voices blend,
A harmony that will not end.
With every breath, we come alive,
In luminescent whispers, we thrive.

Views from the Heart

From mountain tops to valleys deep,
The heart holds views that secrets keep.
In every beat, a story flows,
Of joy and sorrow, highs and lows.

With open arms, we embrace the dawn,
Each moment cherished, never gone.
In every glance, connections weave,
A tapestry of love we believe.

Through laughter shared and tear-streaked grace,
Our journeys shape this sacred space.
Views from the heart, illuminated bright,
Guide us gently into the night.

The Heights of Memory

In peaks of time, the echoes call,
Fragments of joy, shadows that stall.
With every breath, the past unfolds,
In heights of memory, stories told.

Through laughter ringing, moments shine,
In threads of gold, our lives entwine.
Though years may fade, the essence stays,
In the heart's chamber, time obeys.

We climb each step with mindful grace,
In the realm where memories trace.
The heights we scale, a tribute dear,
To all we've loved, all we hold near.

Verses in the Clouds

Whispers drift in a gentle breeze,
Softly carried between the trees.
Nature's canvas, bright and clear,
A symphony for all to hear.

Fluffy shapes in the endless sky,
Floating dreams as they pass by.
Crimson sunsets paint the day,
In the clouds where thoughts can play.

Morning light begins to rise,
Awakens hues in golden ties.
In each formation, stories blend,
A tale of hope that knows no end.

So let us gaze, lose track of time,
Find our peace in nature's rhyme.
With every wisp and every glow,
In the clouds, our spirits flow.

Echoes from the Heights

Mountains tall, their whispers call,
To those who seek beyond the fall.
In the distance, echoes reign,
A chorus sung through sun and rain.

Footsteps light on rugged stone,
In the silence, we're not alone.
Voices carried on the wind,
In these heights, our hearts rescind.

Stars above twinkle bright,
Guiding souls through the endless night.
In the shadow, dreams take flight,
Carried forth by the moon's soft light.

With every step, the world unveils,
A tapestry of ancient tales.
In the heights, we come alive,
In the echoes, spirits thrive.

Dusk's Embrace on the Town

As the day begins to fade,
Shadows stretch where light has played.
Soft glow of streetlamps ignites,
Whispers dance in the cool nights.

Café chatter fills the air,
Laughter lingers everywhere.
Windows flicker with a glow,
In the dusk, our hearts bestow.

Moonlit paths in silent grace,
Every corner, a warm embrace.
Under stars, we roam and dream,
In this moment, we are seen.

Dusk, the painter of the sky,
Coloring life as we pass by.
In the town where memories stay,
Night unfolds, and dreams hold sway.

The Language of Neon Dreams

Neon lights in vibrant hues,
Paint the night with electric blues.
Stories told in colors bright,
Illuminating dark with light.

Each sign speaks, a bold refrain,
Whispered hopes in this domain.
Dreamers walk with eyes aglow,
In this world, our spirits flow.

Reflections dance on rain-slick streets,
Echoes of laughter that time repeats.
Life ignites in a heartbeat's pace,
In the neon's warm embrace.

With every pulse, the city breathes,
Weaving tales among the leaves.
In this language, dreams align,
In neon glow, our hearts entwine.

Reflections Over Rooftops

The sun dips low, a warm embrace,
Shadows stretch across the space.
Windows glint like scattered stars,
Whispers echo from afar.

City hums a gentle tune,
Crickets sing beneath the moon.
Life unfolds in every gleam,
A tapestry of hopes and dreams.

With every breath, a story told,
Of lovers young and hearts of old.
A canvas bright with life's detail,
In twilight's light, we set our sail.

Rooftops hold the secrets near,
In their heights, we face our fear.
With each sunset, dreams take flight,
On the edge of day and night.

The Balance of Nature and Man

In harmony, we seek our place,
Nature's touch, a warm embrace.
Mountains rise, and rivers flow,
A dance of life, a gentle show.

In shadows deep, the forest breathes,
While human hands pull at the leaves.
With every stone that we displace,
We risk the bond, our sacred space.

But in the stillness, hope does grow,
A seed of change we plant, we sow.
With wisdom's heart, we learn to stand,
Together strong, nature and man.

A bridge we build, a path we share,
In every heartbeat, show we care.
Rekindle trust, let spirits blend,
In balance seek the change we send.

In the Embrace of Altitude

High above, where eagles soar,
In the clouds, we seek for more.
Mountains whisper tales untold,
In their arms, we find our bold.

The breeze carries a lonesome tune,
Beneath the sun, beneath the moon.
With every step, the earth we climb,
In silence speaks the voice of time.

With vistas wide, our spirits rise,
Through valleys deep, to boundless skies.
In solitude, we find our peace,
In elevation, our hearts release.

Yet fragile is this lofty dream,
For nature holds a hidden seam.
In height's embrace, we learn to tread,
With reverence for the trails we've led.

Urban Legends of the Night

Underneath the city's glow,
Whispers linger, tales in tow.
Echoed footsteps down the street,
Secrets trade in shadows sweet.

The midnight train, a ghostly call,
Flickering lights, the passing thrall.
Stories twist through alleys dark,
In every corner hides a spark.

Fabled figures haunt the skies,
As moonlit magic softly lies.
With every glance, the past returns,
In urban legends, the heart yearns.

So listen close when night descends,
To lore where truth and fiction blends.
For in the stillness, myths ignite,
And dance among the stars so bright.

Metrical Moments at the Peak

At dawn's first light, the summit glows,
Whispers of wind in gentle flows.
Nature's rhythm, a heartbeats' song,
In every moment, we all belong.

Climbing heights, where silence sings,
Embracing peace that nature brings.
Sky and earth in soft embrace,
A perfect stillness, a sacred space.

Clouds drift by like fleeting dreams,
Floating thoughts on sunlit beams.
Each step taken, a journey true,
In the heart of the wild, we renew.

With every peak, a story told,
Of adventures brave, of spirits bold.
In this realm where silence reigns,
We find our souls, and leave our chains.

Twilight's Urban Lullaby

City lights twinkle in the dusk,
As day gives way to night's calm musk.
In hushed whispers, stories flow,
As evening blankets the urban glow.

Concrete jungles, shadows cast,
Dreams and hopes in silence vast.
Amidst the hustle, we find repose,
In twilight's arms, where comfort grows.

Each corner holds a fleeting sigh,
Underneath the velvet sky.
Trains rumble softly, time stands still,
Captured moments, sweet and thrill.

As stars awaken, the world slows down,
In twilight's serenade, we wear our crown.
Together we whisper, hearts alive,
Finding solace where dreamers thrive.

Flights of Fancy in the City

Dreams take wing on asphalt streams,
In bustling streets, the heart still beams.
Skyscrapers rise, where eagles might soar,
In every corner, magic to explore.

Children laugh, their spirits free,
In playgrounds bright, where joy's a spree.
Adventurers roam with stars in their eyes,
Carving their paths to endless skies.

Cafés hum with chatter and cheer,
As stories unfold, year after year.
Nightfall wraps the city in dreams,
While quiet moments slip through seams.

Lovers stroll beneath soft streetlights,
Each whispered promise soft as flights.
In these moments, we all grow wise,
Flights of fancy beneath urban skies.

Glimpses of the Infinite

In a world so vast, we seek the light,
Stars above, our guiding sight.
Galaxies dance in boundless space,
Whispers of time in a timeless grace.

Each heartbeat echoes, softly profound,
In the silence, all truths are found.
Mysteries linger in shadows deep,
Glimpses of wonders that never sleep.

Through the cosmos, we drift and sway,
Infinite tales of night and day.
In every heartbeat, the universe sings,
A reminder of all the love that it brings.

With open hearts, we gaze above,
Seeking the stars, the essence of love.
In fleeting moments, eternity lies,
In glimpses of infinite, we rise.

Tales from the Towering Heights

In the glow of the rising sun,
Whispers of dreams have begun.
Steel and stone reach for the sky,
While eagles above gracefully fly.

Voices echo in the breeze,
Stories weave through ancient trees.
From balconies, hopes cascade,
In shadows, legends are made.

Windows gleam with longing eyes,
Each pane a glimpse of the prize.
Stairwells echo with the past,
In this fortress, memories vast.

Yet in the height, we find our place,
In every corner, a warm embrace.
Tales are told and hearts ignite,
In the tower's arms, dreams take flight.

Lyrical Murmurs of the Urban Heart

Beneath the city's vibrant hum,
Rhythms pulse, the future's drum.
Concrete jungles rise and fall,
In every heartbeat, hear the call.

Neon lights flicker and dance,
Every shadow holds a chance.
Voices meld in rich refrain,
Hopes and dreams intertwined with pain.

Pavement whispers secrets low,
In alleyways, stories flow.
Laughter bursts from crowded streets,
In the chaos, life repeats.

Mirrored faces, transient souls,
Chasing moments, seeking goals.
In the fabric of this place,
Lyrical murmurs leave their trace.

Reflections on High

Where the clouds kiss the peaks,
Silent thoughts grow, wisdom speaks.
Mountains stand with timeless grace,
Ancient echoes they embrace.

Rivers shimmer, trails entwine,
Nature's beauty, pure and fine.
In stillness, we ponder and muse,
In solitude, we often choose.

The summit calls with a gentle hand,
Leading us to a promised land.
Every step a story spun,
Reflections whisper, 'You have won.'

Beneath the vast, unending sky,
Our spirits soar, yearning high.
In each breath, the world aligns,
In reflections, truth defines.

The Light Between Buildings

In narrow spaces where shadows fall,
A flicker of hope illuminates all.
Between the bricks, stories bloom,
In the quiet, dispelling gloom.

Sunbeams dance on pavement cracks,
In the heart of the city's tracks.
Beneath the arch of twilight's grace,
Memories linger, time can't erase.

Whispers of dreams fill the air,
Lighting paths with gentle care.
In each moment, connections spark,
Illuminating the unseen mark.

Together we walk, side by side,
Finding warmth where shadows abide.
In the glow, we stand as one,
In the light between buildings, we run.

Shadows Stretching Along the Sidelines

In the fading light, shadows play,
Dancing softly, they drift away.
Whispers linger in the night,
As the world dims, out of sight.

Figures blend with the twilight,
Echoes calling, soft and slight.
A hush falls over the land,
As time slips through like grains of sand.

Footprints trace a forgotten tale,
In the stillness, dreams set sail.
Beneath the arch of endless skies,
Mysteries linger, no goodbyes.

Embers glow where hearts once burned,
In this quiet, the world's turned.
Each shadow holds a secret deep,
In the night's embrace, we keep.

City Dreams Beneath the Stars

Lights flicker like distant stars,
Dreams are born behind steel bars.
Voices echo through the streets,
As the city's heartbeat beats.

In the corners, hopes collide,
Stories woven, hearts confide.
Each window tells a tale unique,
In every shadow, secrets peek.

Sky above, so vast, so bright,
Guides the lost through the night.
In the chaos, a subtle grace,
Where every soul finds their place.

With every dream that takes its flight,
New horizons spark delight.
Underneath the cosmic veil,
City dreams will never pale.

Metropolis Musings

Beneath the towers, time stands still,
Concrete giants set against the thrill.
Stories echo with each footstep,
In this labyrinth, emotions leapt.

People hurry, a constant race,
In the hustle, they find their space.
Above, the skyline sings a tune,
Under the watchful, glowing moon.

Moments captured in fleeting glances,
Life unfolds in second chances.
Amidst the rush, a stillness finds,
In the chaos, peace unwinds.

Metropolis whispers, softly sweet,
Every heartbeat, every street.
Through it all, we weave and blend,
In this city, we transcend.

A Serenade to the Skyline

The skyline's silhouette at dusk,
Glistening dreams, a vibrant musk.
Colors dance as the sun retreats,
Painting stories where twilight meets.

On rooftops high, we catch the breeze,
In every heart, a longing frees.
Stars appear like whispers faint,
A serenade, the night's quaint.

Echoes of laughter fill the air,
As memories fold, layer by layer.
With every glance at the cosmic expanse,
Life invites us to take a chance.

A serenade to the skyline vast,
Reminds us of futures, tethered to past.
In every breath, a dream takes flight,
Under the shimmer of distant light.

Celestial Narratives

Stars whisper secrets, glowing bright,
In the deep azure of the night.
Constellations weave tales from afar,
Guided by the light of each wandering star.

Moonlit dreams drift on gentle streams,
Veiled in shadows, where starlight gleams.
Galaxies spin in a cosmic dance,
Of love and hope, they take their chance.

Eclipses show the dark and the light,
Moments lost, yet shining bright.
Planets align in a celestial tune,
Harmonious echoes beneath the moon.

Across the skies, our souls take flight,
In celestial narratives, bold and bright.
Woven in time, our stories soar,
Forever written in the cosmic lore.

Melodies in the Mist

Softly the fog blankets the ground,
Whispers of nature, sweetly profound.
Birds sing softly, a lullaby's grace,
Melodies in the mist, a tranquil space.

Waves of sound in the hazy air,
Echoes of laughter, a chorus fair.
The morning unfolds, colors arise,
As dew-kissed petals greet the skies.

Gentle breezes through branches sway,
Nature's orchestra in a grand ballet.
Harmonies dance on a silver stream,
In this moment, we live the dream.

Every note a story untold,
In the mist, mysteries unfold.
Breathe in deep, let your heart persist,
Finding peace in melodies mist.

Cityscapes in Verse

Call of the city in twilight's glow,
Streets alive with stories to show.
Buildings towering, reaching high,
Beneath the canvas of a painted sky.

Sidewalks teeming with dreams untold,
Stitching the fabric of young and old.
Neon lights in a vibrant spree,
Whispers of hope in the urban sea.

Trains rumble like a heartbeat strong,
Echoing life, a dynamic song.
Corners adorned with laughter and tears,
Chronicles woven through the years.

Cityscapes dance in a vibrant trance,
A pulsing rhythm, a lively chance.
In every shadow and every beam,
Lies the essence of a shared dream.

Haikus of the Heights

Mountains stand so tall,
Whispers of the wind call out,
Bridging earth and sky.

Clouds drift like soft dreams,
Kissing peaks with gentle grace,
Nature's pure embrace.

Sunrise paints the world,
Golden hues on snow-capped crowns,
A new day unfolds.

Stars wink from above,
Silent witnesses of time,
In the night, we soar.

City Lights and Lullabies

Neon glows in twilight's grasp,
A city hums, a pulsing clasp.
Stars peer down through smoky haze,
While dreams are stitched in velvet ways.

Echoes dance on busy streets,
As life unfolds in whispered beats.
Horns and laughter fill the air,
In these moments, we lay bare.

Soft lullabies from windows sway,
Cradling hearts at end of day.
Among the chaos, peace will bloom,
In city life, we find our room.

So move with rhythm, lose the fight,
Embrace the magic of city light.
For in its glow, we are alive,
In every shadow, dreams survive.

The Height of Inspiration

Above the clouds where eagles soar,
Ideas spark, ignite, and roar.
With every peak that we ascend,
New visions rise, our minds transcend.

The wind whispers tales of old,
Inspire boldness, dreamers unfold.
Mountains echo with every thought,
In heights unknown, our battles fought.

Pen poised high, we chase the breeze,
Crafting words like rustling leaves.
At the summit, we pause to see,
The beauty born from being free.

With hope our guide, we navigate,
Embrace the journey, leave the weight.
For inspiration's call is clear,
In every heart that dares to steer.

Serenades from Above

Moonlight spills on tranquil seas,
As lullabies drift on the breeze.
Stars align in velvet skies,
Whispering dreams that never die.

A serenade from realms unknown,
Soft notes linger, gently honed.
Angelic voices fill the night,
Guiding wanderers in their flight.

From mountain tops to oceans wide,
Nature sings, a faithful guide.
Harmony in every breath,
A symphony that conquers death.

In the stillness, hearts awake,
To serenades that love can make.
With every note, we find our way,
In music's arms, we long to stay.

Conversations Under the Stars

In the hush of twilight's glow,
Two souls meet where starlight flows.
Whispers linger in the night,
As secrets shared take gentle flight.

Moonbeams lit on soft embrace,
Time stands still, we find our space.
Questions rise like fireflies,
In the darkness, truth belies.

With every glance, the world fades away,
In this moment, we choose to stay.
The cosmos listens, hearts reveal,
In these talks, we learn to feel.

Conversations woven in the stars,
Unravel time and heal old scars.
So let us linger through the night,
Under skies where dreams take flight.

Serenade of Steel and Glass

In a city where dreams are framed,
Steel towers rise, their beauty claimed.
Reflections dance in the fading light,
A serenade whispers through the night.

Echoes of footsteps, a rhythmic embrace,
Glass facades hold stories we chase.
Each corner a canvas, each street a song,
In this urban realm, we all belong.

The skyline hums with a vibrant pulse,
Life rushes by in its seamless repulse.
Yet in the chaos, a quiet space,
Where steel and glass come to interlace.

So pause for a moment, breathe in the scene,
Let the city's symphony weave through the dream.
In a serenade of steel and glass,
Find your rhythm, let each moment pass.

Evening Canopy

Beneath the twilight's gentle glow,
Whispers of night begin to flow.
Trees stretch high, a leafy dome,
In this tranquil space, we find our home.

Stars emerge, like diamonds rare,
Glimmers of hope in the evening air.
Crickets sing their serenade sweet,
As shadows gather, time feels complete.

The breeze carries tales from afar,
Secrets spun in the light of a star.
Nature's embrace, a soothing sigh,
Under the canvas of the vast sky.

In this sanctuary, dreams take flight,
Evening's canopy, a lullaby light.
Together we wander, hand in hand,
In the hush of the night, forever we stand.

Metro Musings

In the belly of the city, we rush and align,
Strangers' faces, stories entwine.
A symphony plays in the rumble below,
Life in the metro, a vibrant flow.

Time ticks softly on the aging tracks,
Memories linger, then fade into black.
Each stop a moment, each journey a thread,
Connected in silence, where words go unsaid.

Rattling carriages echo our dreams,
Hope springs eternal from the unseen seams.
A nod, a smile, a shared glance in the crowd,
In this metal cocoon, we are both lost and found.

So we ride through the tunnels, a fleeting delight,
Metro musings guide us through the night.
In the heart of the city, quick silver and steel,
We capture the moments, the pulse of the real.

The Language of Heights

Atop the peaks where the eagles soar,
The language of heights beckons us more.
Whispers of winds carve paths in the sky,
Speaking in silence, where spirits fly.

Mountains stand tall, ancient and wise,
Guardian sentinels under vast skies.
Their shadows stretch, a canvas of time,
Each summit reached feels like a rhyme.

Clouds drift softly, a shroud of dreams,
Nature's enchantment flows through the beams.
The world below fades in the expanse,
Here in the heights, we find our chance.

With every breath, we draw in the light,
The language of heights, our souls take flight.
A journey unfolds where the heart learns to see,
In the arms of the mountains, we are truly free.

Urban Ballads at Dusk

The city hums with twilight's glow,
Streetlights blink, a vibrant show.
Voices echo, dreams take flight,
In the heart of the urban night.

Skyscrapers loom, shadows cast,
Moments fleeting, memories last.
Faint laughter peels through the air,
Whispers of lives beyond compare.

Waves of traffic, a constant stream,
Each face lost in their own dream.
The rhythm pulses, a steady beat,
As footsteps dance on concrete street.

In this city where stories blend,
We find new paths and old friends.
Under the sky, a canvas wide,
These urban ballads never hide.

A Canvas of Concrete and Stars

Beneath the skyline's jagged lines,
A thousand dreams, a thousand signs.
Concrete jungles reaching high,
While stars peek through, shy on the fly.

Whispers of night bring tales anew,
Of love and loss, of hopes that grew.
Each alley tells a vivid tale,
Where shadows dance and spirits sail.

Graffiti murals splashed with flair,
A canvas alive in midnight air.
Every heartbeat, a brushstroke bold,
Stories painted, waiting to be told.

Skyward gazes, we catch a spark,
In this city, nothing feels stark.
A blend of dreams, both near and far,
On this canvas of concrete and stars.

The Rhythm of City Lights

Neon signs flicker, catching the night,
The pulse of the city, electric delight.
Each corner whispers, tales to unfold,
In luminous lanes, life is bold.

Cars rush past in a shimmering stream,
Every moment alive, every moment a dream.
Children laugh, lovers entwined,
The rhythm of city lights, so perfectly timed.

A symphony rises, horns and feet,
A celebration of chaos, a bustling beat.
Stars above, dimmed by the gleam,
In this vibrant maze, we chase every dream.

As shadows lengthen and colors fade,
The city's heartbeat, never afraid.
Under the glow, we find our part,
In the rhythm of city lights, we start.

Beneath the Painted Horizon

Sunset spills colors, a dreamy blend,
While day gently bows, night starts to send.
Hues of fire in the fading light,
A painted horizon, bold and bright.

The whispers of dusk, a calming tune,
As stars awaken, one by one, soon.
Fading footsteps on the gravel path,
In twilight's embrace, we feel its warmth.

The sky transforms, a canvas so vast,
Every heartbeat, echoes of the past.
We gather hopes and let them fly,
Under the gaze of the evening sky.

Life unfolds in the softest embrace,
In nocturnal wonder, we find our place.
Beneath this painted horizon wide,
We dream our dreams, no need to hide.

Rhythms of the Rooftops

Underneath the vast blue skies,
We dance where the skyline lies.
Echoes of laughter fill the air,
A symphony of life laid bare.

Chimneys rise like sentinels tall,
Whispers of dreams silently call.
Each rooftop tells a tale untold,
In the warmth of the sun's soft gold.

Birds weave melodies through the breeze,
Carrying secrets among the trees.
The city hums, a vibrant tune,
As day surrenders to the moon.

In dusk's embrace, shadows fall,
Mirroring the night's sweet thrall.
Where heartbeats sync with the stars,
We find our rhythm among the cars.

Whispers of the Highrise

In the heights where dreams ascend,
Voices of the skyline blend.
Windows glimmer like shooting stars,
Guardians of our hopes and scars.

Each floor a world of silent tales,
Weaving through the crowded trails.
The air is thick with bustling light,
Chasing shadows, embracing night.

Balconies adorned with vibrant blooms,
Life flourishes amidst the glooms.
Each whisper calls from within,
Strength found where our tales begin.

Heartbeats echo in concrete halls,
The pulse of hope, it gently calls.
From heights above, we watch it grow,
In the twilight's golden glow.

Poetry in Concrete

Amidst the stone and silent grey,
Life unfolds in its own way.
Stories etched in every crack,
A canvas where the dreams unpack.

Sidewalks sing beneath our feet,
Rhythms of the city beat.
Lost in thoughts, we wander far,
Each moment is a twinkling star.

Graffiti blooms like wildflowers,
Transforming bricks to vibrant towers.
In this jungle made of steel,
We find the lost, the raw, the real.

Voices echo in alleyways,
Resilience shines through weary days.
Each corner holds a hidden tune,
Underneath the watchful moon.

Elevated Stanzas

Up above where dreams take flight,
We gather 'neath the city light.
Words ascend like kites in spring,
Soaring high on freedom's wing.

In every line, a story grows,
As vibrant as the city glows.
Time stands still in thoughtful pause,
Embracing life without a cause.

From busy streets to quiet views,
We pen our hopes with every muse.
Lines connect like hearts entwined,
In elevated thoughts, we find.

The poetry of city life,
In rhythms sharp and subtle strife.
Each stanza crafted with great care,
A testament to dreams we share.

Where Dreams Touch the Skies

Underneath the starlit haze,
Wishes dance in gentle ways.
Clouds like whispers float so high,
Where our dreams learn how to fly.

In the quiet of the night,
Stars will guide with sparkling light.
Every heartbeat sings a tune,
Beneath the watchful, silver moon.

Cascading hopes begin to rise,
Paint the canvas of the skies.
With each dawn, new lives commence,
In the realm of innocence.

Hand in hand, we dare to dream,
Life's a vast and vibrant stream.
Together, we will chart the course,
Where our souls embrace their force.

Phrases of the Paved Path

Footsteps echo on the ground,
As stories of the lost are found.
Every stone, a tale to tell,
Of hopes that rise and fear that fell.

In the alleys, whispers weave,
Secrets that the shadows leave.
Each corner holds a fleeting glance,
Inviting hearts to take a chance.

With every stride, a new refrain,
Voices blend like gentle rain.
Life's a journey, not a race,
In each moment, we find our place.

Together, we will walk this road,
Sharing dreams, a heavy load.
In the spaces in between,
Every step fulfills a dream.

Midnight Musings in the Metropolis

Neon lights like stars aglow,
Busy streets where dreamers flow.
In the city's heart, we seek,
Words unspoken find their peak.

Silent thoughts, a gentle hum,
Thoughts like music yet to come.
In the hush of midnight's grace,
We discover our true place.

Concrete jungles thick and tall,
Whispers rise above it all.
Flickering signs and distant sounds,
In this maze, our hope abounds.

As the world takes a pause and breathes,
Magic stirs beneath the leaves.
In the night, our spirits soar,
Crafting dreams forevermore.

The Art of Elevated Dreams

On the canvas of the night,
We paint our dreams in colors bright.
With every brush stroke, we unveil,
A world where hope will never fail.

Floating high above the ground,
Whispers of the heart resound.
In the realms of purest grace,
We find our true and sacred space.

Each vibrant hue, a wish in flight,
In our hands, the world ignites.
Crafted visions, bold and clear,
Calling forth what we hold dear.

So let our spirits intertwine,
In the art of dreams, we'll shine.
Painting futures, hand in hand,
Together in this promised land.

Bards of the Skyline

Whispers of steel and glass arise,
Echoes of songs beneath the skies.
Crafted by hands that dream and dare,
Melodies linger in the city air.

Voices of ages drift through the night,
Serenading stars, burning bright.
Each note a story, a memory spun,
In harmony with the setting sun.

From rooftops high, the tales are told,
Of dreams that shimmer and hearts of gold.
With every chord, a pulse of life,
In the dance of joy, in the strife.

So let the bards with voices clear,
Chant to the skyline, year after year.
For in their songs, we find our place,
An eternal bond with time and space.

Notes from the Nebula

In the cradle of stars, a soft sigh waits,
Whispers of dust and cosmic fates.
Galaxies swirl in a gentle embrace,
Carving their secrets in dark, spacious space.

Celestial hymns rise from the void,
Notes of creation, softly deployed.
Each twinkling light, a story to share,
An orchestra playing in the cool, night air.

Patterns unfold in luminous hues,
Painting the darkness with radiant views.
The symphony plays through the ages long,
Echoing softly, a celestial song.

So let us listen to the night's refrain,
As stars spin tales of joy and pain.
In this concert grand of time and space,
We find our purpose, our sacred place.

Dawn's Palette

Softly the light breaks through the night,
Painting the world in hues of delight.
Crimson and gold embrace the sky,
As day awakens with a gentle sigh.

Brush of the sun, so warm and bold,
Stirring the dreams, the stories untold.
Nature unfolds in vibrant display,
Greeting the dawn of a brand new day.

Whispers of morning dance on the breeze,
Kissing the petals on waking trees.
Each flower, a note in sun's grand song,
Celebrating life, where we all belong.

So join the chorus that nature intends,
Embrace the sunrise, where shadows end.
In dawn's embrace, our spirits rise,
With every color that lights the skies.

Vertical Reveries

Towering dreams stretch towards the blue,
Reaching for heights, where hopes renew.
Each step we climb, a whisper clear,
On the path of ambition, devoid of fear.

Walls of concrete and metal gleam,
Reflecting the vision, the fervent dream.
A symphony of voices, rising high,
In vertical realms, where we dare fly.

Gravity holds no sway on the heart,
As we navigate the mind's great art.
Through windowed views of the world below,
In the chase of dreams, our spirits grow.

So let us ascend, let courage ignite,
In the realms of hopes, where we find flight.
With each new height, we embrace the thrill,
In vertical reveries, we conquer still.

Milton Keynes UK
Ingram Content Group UK Ltd.
UKHW020119221024
449869UK00010B/341